WOMEN
IN POSITIONS
OF LEADERSHIP

WOMEN
IN POSITIONS
OF LEADERSHIP

LENA KOYA AND NANCY FURSTINGER

New York

Published in 2018 by The Rosen Publishing Group, Inc.
29 East 21st Street, New York, NY 10010

Library of Congress Cataloging-in-Publication Data

Names: Koya, Lena, author. | Furstinger, Nancy, author.
Title: Women in positions of leadership / Lena Koya and Nancy Furstinger.
Description: New York : Rosen Publishing, 2018. | Series: Women in the world |
Includes bibliographical references and index. | Audience: Grades 7–12.
Identifiers: LCCN 2017017479 | ISBN 9781508177166 (library bound) | ISBN 9781508178590 (paperback)
Subjects: LCSH: Leadership in women.
Classification: LCC HQ1236 .K694 2018 | DDC 303.3/4082—dc23
LC record available at https://lccn.loc.gov/2017017479

Manufactured in China

CONTENTS

oday, women are making history as leaders in the corporate world, politics, and beyond. But women have always taken on leadership roles that have changed our world for the better. And yet often their accomplishments have been downplayed or ignored and the spotlight has instead focused on men's achievements.

In many societies across the world, women are seen as displaying fewer leadership qualities than men. This is because women are often encouraged in these societies to be more demure and less assertive, while men are encouraged to take on more leadership characteristics. These messages that society sends girls and young women can be damaging. They tell them that they will struggle to become the heads of companies or one day dream of becoming the leaders of their countries. These messages are not only damaging, but they are untrue. In fact, innate leadership abilities are not dependent on one's gender or biological sex. And, even if someone is not born with some of these typical leadership qualities, they can be developed. This book will show teens how.

Even if someone is not born with typical leadership qualities, leadership characteristics such as confidence and assertiveness can be developed.

Leadership abilities, such as extroversion, charisma, and assertiveness, can be developed through participating in extracurricular activities, team sports, or community volunteering. Confidence can be developed in these activities, which can be key to taking on future leadership positions. Young women can also be encouraged to develop their communication skills and interpersonal skills to draw people together—a key component of leadership ability.

But developing leadership skills is also about looking to role models. Emulating female leaders who have successfully reached the summit of their careers is a great way to put oneself on the path. These women trailblazers have paved the way for other generations of women to follow their lead. It's also a good idea to look a bit closer to home for role models. Young women can look to the older women in their own lives as mentors, and seek them out for advice about balancing their career and personal lives, managing teams, and seeking out the promotions and pay that they deserve.

Leaders are not all born or made. They do not all follow a particular management style, and they do not have to be extroverted or aggressive. But good leaders know the value of teamwork, communication, and listening. Good leaders know that it is not all about them, but about the people who will carry out their vision. They know that it is ultimately about not only themselves, but about the people with whom they surround themselves.

This book provides guidance for young women to build their own communities of leadership. It offers steps to develop leadership traits and advice for young women looking to become entrepreneurs, politicians, or take on any other leadership role. Perhaps most importantly, it points young women in the direction of past and potential female role models and mentors. Nothing would be possible for any aspiring young leader without them.

CHAPTER 1

WHAT MAKES A LEADER?

People define leadership in different ways. Leadership can mean someone who is willing to take the reins of a group and direct people toward a common goal. It can mean being confident and charismatic and creating a following among people. It can also mean being a good listener and understanding what your team needs to achieve its best. With all of these definitions, leadership always involves bringing people together to work toward a common goal—and not necessarily just being in charge.

Perhaps you've heard the saying, "Great leaders are made, not born." According to an article in *Psychology Today*, "leadership is about

Leadership can mean many different things to different people. However, the goal of leadership is to bring different people together toward a common goal.

one-third born and two-thirds made." Successful leadership can be developed. Although we are all born with the potential to lead, leadership traits require practice to develop, just like anything in life.

However, leadership isn't taught in school. Rather, it takes place by studying the behavior of healthy role models and practicing it on one's own. This is good news for young women who aspire to achieve positions of leadership.

Some qualities that are inherent in a person's nature can be connected with leadership. Of course, it doesn't hurt to be born with "the right stuff." Naturally, successful leaders must be smart. However, they are not necessarily the brainy types who get straight A's. Instead, social intelligence, or the ability to form rewarding relationships with people, is equally if not more important. Another hallmark of leadership is the willingness to take calculated risks. Leaders who are naturally confident and assertive are usually unafraid to take necessary chances, such as going for the basketball team tryouts, to achieve their goals.

Many of these self-assured individuals are extroverts, or people who thrive on social interaction. However, introverts can also find success in leadership positions. Remember, two-thirds of leadership is made, not born. With the desire and will, anyone can grab the leadership reins to overcome any challenges they may have.

QUALITIES OF EFFECTIVE LEADERS

Successful leaders possess a certain set of skills that most other people lack. They are charismatic and creative. They can manage time and people well. They are ambitious and determined, yet ethical and respectful.

Effective leaders have a clear sense of direction. They analyze situations before making decisions and attempting to solve conflicts. They are flexible, with the ability to see alternative points of view, yet are disciplined when called for. They demonstrate a zest for change.

Leadership is a constant learning curve. Good leaders are always gaining new skills and growing from their experiences. Both successes and failures help to shape leaders, making them stronger. Leaders seek feedback from others so they can handle situations more effectively. This helps them to become better problem-solvers, which is one of the most important leadership traits.

Leaders, naturally, need followers. They should communicate their strong vision of the future and motivate followers to believe in them. The best leaders lead by example. They must know when to step aside and delegate responsibility, or hand the job over to someone more capable or able. Strong leaders rely on the strengths of their team to help make decisions and tackle projects. They always give credit to others for their accomplishments.

GENDER AND LEADERSHIP STYLES

Effective leaders share a variety of traits. Due to societal gender norms, however, it can be common for men and women to have different leadership styles. When Dr. Alice Eagly, a scholar on gender and leadership, did a study comparing two distinct styles of leadership, she discovered that men and women possess different qualities. She used two schools of leadership theory to explore how leaders approach power.

TRANSFORMATIONAL LEADERSHIP

Transformational leaders focus on followers, inspiring them to achieve extraordinary outcomes. They awaken team spirit with their enthusiasm. In the process, followers grow and develop their own leadership potential. The leaders transform

Transformational leaders inspire team members to achieve their goals together by focusing on their team instead of their followers by motivating them to achieve top levels of performance.

This type of leader has high standards. Followers admire, respect, and trust their leader as the ideal role model. The leader can be counted on to do the right thing.

Transformational leaders focus on their followers, gaining their trust and confidence. They give personal and undivided attention. Their concern and interest helps coax out top performances from their followers.

Transformational leaders also concentrate on goals and plans to achieve those goals. They paint an optimistic vision of the future. They challenge their followers to share in this vision by taking new and original approaches.

TRANSACTIONAL LEADERSHIP

By contrast, transactional leaders focus on keeping the chain of command clear. These leaders reward their followers for meeting objectives. They discipline their followers when they don't follow procedures. They correct followers when they don't play by the rules.

This type of leader expects followers to follow instructions to complete projects and perform their jobs. Leaders use established methods to manage their followers. They do not encourage creativity or innovative solutions to problems.

LEADERSHIP THAT INSPIRES

Which type of leader do you think coaxes better performances from followers? Which type would inspire and empower you? Research shows that transformational leaders come out on top. The qualities they possess are associated with success. They stimulate their followers to perform better on the job. Their followers report better job satisfaction. Since this type of leader holds positive expectations, followers give their all. They try as hard as possible to succeed.

Female leaders, according to Eagly, are generally more transformational than male leaders. In particular, they are more likely offer more encouragement and support to their followers. They also generally engage in more rewarding behaviors and provide more positive incentives. And they lead by encouraging followers to participate and collaborate on decision-making. Female leaders inspire others to think outside the box.

All of these findings, Eagly writes, "add up to a startling conclusion" about which gender in general is better suited to lead today's corporations. She states that "women's approaches are the more generally

Women often have important leadership qualities that can

effective—while men's often are only somewhat effective or actually hinder effectiveness."

Dr. Bernard Bass, a leadership scholar, agrees that women have an edge over men in this way. He writes, "By the year 2034 the majority of high-level leaders will be women, based on their more transformational qualities." Men who use a transactional leadership style and who aspire to become twenty-first century leaders will need to learn how to adapt.

Leadership in girls can be developed in a variety of ways. Girls should participate in plans of action to achieve goals in their communities and schools. They should be boosted through family support. They should be hands-on—involved in developing, directing, and organizing. Girls should be encouraged to speak out when they witness unfair or unjust treatment. They should learn how to think critically. They should solve problems using creative solutions. They should believe in themselves and their ability to make a difference. Then they should

GENDERED ROLES IN LEADERSHIP

The differences that Dr. Alice Eagly studies in regard to male and female leaders are not due to biological difference. This means that men are not naturally born to be a certain kind of leader, while women are born to be a different kind. Rather, the leadership roles that men and women take on are largely determined by the society they live in. Oftentimes, women are encouraged to be more communicative than men in Western societies because of the way these societies view the role of women. Male leaders may not be taught, through societal messages and role models, to be as communicative, but rather to dictate rules that their team must follow. Also, the organization of businesses—and the expectations of colleagues and others—also mold how men and women may behave differently in leadership positions. Management scholar Rosabeth Moss Kanter has also studied male and female leadership and has found that differences in leadership styles may be due to the way companies are organized and the imbalance of men and women in corporate leadership roles. According to Kanter, when women reach around 40 percent of workforce leadership, their leadership styles may not differ as much from the leadership styles of men.

"play it forward" by mentoring younger girls to help grow their leadership skills.

BUILDING BLOCKS TO LEADERSHIP

As you navigate the path to leadership, you'll need to acquire a group of skills. Here are some suggestions to help develop your leadership style:

1. Leaders are great listeners. You should concentrate more on listening and less on talking. Listen with full attention to absorb what others are saying. When you do speak, focus on sounding positive and conveying empathy.

2. Keep a daily journal of your accomplishments. Spend five minutes at the end of each day reflecting on events—positive and negative—that stand out in your mind. The small wins will motivate you to move forward. The setbacks will motivate you to work harder so you can conquer similar stumbling blocks.

3. Observe people who have charisma—the ability to charm and influence others. Project confidence through positive body language, a friendly smile, and an enthusiastic voice. Use a professional voice in all types of communications— written and oral.

4. Convey optimism and energy. Show your independence by tackling a new challenge. Learn from mistakes and move on. As you constantly strive for improvement, seek feedback from mentors and those in higher positions.

As you develop your beliefs and values, remember to be true to yourself. A genuine person is more easily trusted by others. Focus on the future by thinking positively. The sky's the limit—you can go far in what you are trying to achieve. Aim for goals that may take effort to attain. Read about role models and careers that inspire you. Explore ways to make your dreams come true.

FEMALE LEADERS AS TRAILBLAZERS

Since recorded history, women have taken on important roles to change their societies for the better. Female rulers, like Hatshepsut of ancient Egypt and Queen Victoria of England, have ruled entire kingdoms for many years and shaped their country's policies for many years after. Others, like Burmese activist Aung San Suu Kyi, have fought for the rights of their people from the sidelines before eventually coming to power. One similarity these different female leaders share is their passion for ushering in change.

Leaders have often come together to lobby for change. They

Sojourner Truth was an influential women's rights activist. She escaped from slavery and went on to fight both for the

know that there is strength in numbers as they support or fight for particular causes. Two generations, or "waves," of women joined forces in the past to secure rights and opportunities for women equal to those of their male counterparts. A third wave is currently encouraging personal empowerment and action for women around the globe.

FEMALE LEADERS OF THE FIRST WAVE

During the nineteenth century the first wave of dynamic leaders emerged during the campaign for women's suffrage, the right for women to vote in public elections. They rebelled against the "cult of true womanhood." This common attitude preached four virtues for women: piety, purity, submission, and domesticity. Instead, the women wanted their own political identities.

It took nearly a century of organized activism for American and Canadian women to win the right to vote. The Nineteenth Amendment to the Constitution, barring any United States citizen to be denied the right to vote based on sex, was ratified in 1920. In Canada, provinces first began legalizing voting rights for women in 1917, with the last province (Québec) joining women's suffrage in 1940. Female citizens were finally victorious.

SOJOURNER TRUTH

One of the earliest women's rights activists was Sojourner Truth (1797–1883). This leader was born into slavery. She eventually escaped to freedom and became a traveling preacher. Truth had dual passions: the abolition of slavery and women's rights. She spoke out on behalf of both.

Perhaps her most famous speech was "Ain't I a Woman?" It was delivered at the Ohio Women's Rights Convention in 1851. Truth dared to speak out after several men attempted to claim that men had the superior intellect. Truth, who was illiterate, spoke from the heart. Her passion made her articulate. She continued to campaign for the rights of women during speaking tours throughout the rest of her life.

ELIZABETH CADY STANTON

Elizabeth Cady Stanton (1815–1902) was another key leader in the fight for women's rights in the United States. Her determination to change the unfair laws under which women lived propelled her into action. She demanded justice for women at the first Woman's Rights Convention in Seneca Falls, New York, in 1848.

Stanton used her skills as a persuasive speaker to call for reforms. She used her talent for writing to

Elizabeth Cady Stanton (*left*) and Susan B. Anthony (*right*) were leaders of the women's suffrage movement in the

pen speeches, letters, pamphlets, articles, and essays. Stanton also used her strong leadership abilities to organize and head the National Woman Suffrage Association (NWSA).

SUSAN B. ANTHONY

Another inspirational leader joined Stanton. Susan B. Anthony (1820–1906) used her negotiating and organization skills to oversee a women's suffrage convention. Starting in 1851, the two women toured the United States giving speeches promoting women's rights. Anthony's leadership qualities thrust her into the spotlight. She was an enthusiastic advocate and a determined worker who was constantly on the go.

Anthony also dealt with problems in a unique way. She decided to challenge the Fourteenth Amendment, which stated that all people born in the United States are citizens and no legal privileges could be denied to any citizen, by registering to vote. Anthony stated that women were citizens and should be allowed the privilege to vote. She tested her premise in 1872 when she cast her vote in the presidential election along with fifteen other women. All were arrested for this illegal action. Only Anthony was brought before a court, where the judge gave his verdict of guilty before the trial even started. Anthony stood by her beliefs. She refused to pay the $100 fine, and no further action was taken against her.

THE FAMOUS FIVE

In Canada, five women—Emily Murphy (1868–1933), Irene Marryat Parlby (1868–1965), Nellie Mooney McClung (1873–1951), Louise Crummy McKinney (1868–1931), and Henrietta Muir Edwards (1849–1931)—stood up to the Supreme Court of Canada in support of women's suffrage in 1927. They filed a petition asking if the word "persons" in the Canadian Constitution included women. These five activists eventually had their question answered in the affirmative upon appeal, creating an important precedent in the continued fight for women's rights and suffrage. In addition to their work as activists, these women went on to lead important political careers in their country. Murphy would become the British Empire's first female judge, Parlby became the first female Cabinet minister in Alberta, and McKinney became the first woman elected to any legislature in Canada and the entire British Empire.

FEMALE LEADERS OF THE SECOND WAVE

Four decades after women won the vote in the United States, a second wave of female trailblazers surfaced in the 1960s. The women's liberation movement, like the suffrage movement, would lead to sweeping social changes not just in the United States, but around the world.

BETTY FRIEDAN

Betty Friedan (1921–2006) ignited the cause of women's liberation in 1963 with her book *The Feminine Mystique*. In its pages she described "the problem that has no name." She wrote about how suburban women felt dissatisfied in a culture that didn't allow them to fulfill their potential. Her groundbreaking book changed the lives of women as they continued their struggle for equality.

Friedan campaigned for an end to discrimination against women. This feminist leader helped found the National Organization for Women (NOW). It was the first major group since the 1920s committed to women's rights. Friedan served as its first president.

NOW lobbied for passage of the Equal Rights Amendment (ERA), which would guarantee "equal justice under law" to both sexes. Despite decades of lobbying, petitioning, rallies, picketing, and civil disobedience, Congress has not yet ratified the ERA.

Friedan continued to demand full equality for American women. She lead more than ten thousand women in a march down New York City's Fifth Avenue during the 1970 Women's Strike for Equality. Friedan was a blunt and brainy leader. However, she alienated some followers with her rude and arrogant manner.

GLORIA STEINEM

Fellow activist Gloria Steinem became the face of the feminist movement in the 1970s. Together with Friedan and other feminists, she formed the National Women's Political Caucus in 1971. This

Gloria Steinem became one of the most recognized leaders of the US feminist movement during the 1970s.

grassroots organization is dedicated to increasing women's participation in politics. The following year, Steinem became the founding editor of *Ms.* magazine, which raised consciousness for thousands of subscribers.

Steinem spoke through the pages of her national publication and at lectures. Some feminists criticized her glamorous image. They questioned whether she could be a committed leader. She fought the backlash by drawing on her inner strength and dedication to social justice. Steinem also relied on the support of other female activists, realizing, like any great leader, that it was impossible to accomplish change alone.

ANGELA DAVIS

Angela Davis became known to millions of Americans when her photo was displayed on the Federal Bureau of Investigation's (FBI) Most Wanted list for her presumed role in the armed takeover of a court in 1971. Davis was not present at the time of the violence, and she was later acquitted of any involvement in the case.

Davis was deeply involved in second-wave feminism, black feminism, and the civil rights movement. She also became an important political figure within the US Communist Party, running for the vice presidency of the United States in 1980 and 1984. Her work, including *Women, Race & Class*, has been inspirational for many black female leaders who came of age during the second wave.

EGYPTIAN TRAILBLAZER: NAWAL EL SAADAWI

Nawal El Saadawi was born in Kafr Tahla, Egypt, in 1931. In 1955, she graduated from Cairo University as a medical doctor. Through her medical work, she met with many Egyptian women and began to talk with them about their experiences as women in a largely patriarchal society. Later, she moved her medical practice to a poorer and more rural area and began to learn more about the hardships Egyptian women faced not just due to their gender, but due to economic status. Eventually, El Saadawi would become the Director of the Ministry of Public Health in Egypt.

Her experiences working with women led her to publish her first book, *Woman and Sex*, in 1972. This became an important second-wave feminist text, and its popularity led to the loss of her position at the Ministry of Public Health. Later, El Saadawi went on to publish a feminist magazine called *Confrontation*. She also founded the Health Education Association and the Egyptian Women Writers' Association. El Saadawi has used her leadership skills to advocate for women's rights in Egypt and around the world, and she often speaks about the hardships women face in

(continued on the next page)

(continued from the previous page)

patriarchal cultures. Her work was deemed dangerous by the Egyptian government in 1981, when she was briefly imprisoned for her activism.

Nawal El Saadawi has held important positions in the Egyptian government and has worked as both a doctor and activist.

THE THIRD WAVE

A third wave of trailblazers surfaced in the 1990s and continues into the twenty-first century. Like the two previous waves, this one works toward social reform in our culture, education, and politics.

The third wave of female leadership is focused on a variety of causes. Young women are encouraged to concentrate their attention on personal empowerment as a starting point for change. Third-wave female leaders also celebrate diversity. The second wave centered on a narrow category of women with similar characteristics: white, middle-class, cisgender, and heterosexual. The new wave incorporates the voices of a variety of young people from all races, religions, genders, sexualities, and economic classes. Third-wave leaders have also focused on the importance of intersectionality, or the ways in which race, gender, and class intersect to form each individual's experience.

NAVIGATING THE LEADERSHIP PATH

All of these female trailblazers shared common traits. First, they wanted to make a difference in society. They had a clear vision of the goals they aspired to accomplish. They weren't afraid to take enormous risks by moving outside of their comfort zones.

These women were self-confident and had a strong drive to achieve. They pursued their plans with energy and persistence. They stayed in control and calmly assessed the situation. They remained optimistic, even while facing failure. They were successful in leading change. They had expertise in influencing and inspiring teams of people to help them.

The leadership skills of these trailblazers are still relevant for modern leaders. By studying these women's strategies, young women can apply their lessons to become better leaders today. These tips will help young women advance while navigating the leadership path:

- **Connect with the correct female mentor.** A mentor will act as a role model, an advisor, and a sounding board. First, search for women with similar goals as you who can offer you insights. Then, target someone you can look up to as an example to emulate. Ideally, she would be at least ten years older than you. She would be someone interested in reaching the pinnacle of her aspirations—the same spot you seek in the future. Your mentor should be someone you respect.
- **Network to make connections and observe other female leaders in action.** Join organizations, both professional and community, to link up with leaders. Take an active role and promote yourself

as an expert in your areas of interest. People will soon recognize you as a leader. You can also link up with others on business-related social networking sites. These professional sites can help you get to the next level in your career, letting you search for jobs and other business opportunities.

- **Seek stimulation to help you develop and grow.** Take continuing education classes. Attend conferences—someday you may lead one. Raise your hand to ask questions. Read the latest business books. Subscribe to trade magazines and newspapers. Sign up for webinars and submit your questions and comments.

- **Keep an upbeat attitude to motivate and inspire others.** When you face a particular challenge, even if others on your team have lost hope or enthusiasm, remain optimistic. You'll face many challenges on your way up the ladder, so try to stay positive.

- **Assess your skills to determine what distinguishes you from your peers.** Then showcase your talents. Promote yourself speaking your thoughts. Demonstrate what your abilities and credentials can do for others. Talk about your aspirations to become a leader in your group. Stand behind your decisions and maintain your vision, whatever that may be.

CHAPTER 3

DEVELOPING LEADERSHIP ABILITIES

Female leaders today have many more opportunities than ever before. Young women are routinely breaking through the old and false stereotypes that stated that women could not be successful leaders or that they simply did not desire to take on leadership roles.

Many young people can develop leadership tools that they will use later in their lives and careers while in school, in their communities, and in afterschool programs. Effective leadership traits can be developed through organizing events, presiding over meetings, volunteering, and taking charge of group activities. Then students can accept assignments based on their individual skills.

Young women can develop their leadership skills through taking part in extracurricular activities and volunteering in their communities.

Today, young women have increasing opportunities to lead in school, which helps build character, poise, and integrity. This allows them to succeed after graduation by winning scholarships, getting accepted into top colleges, and leading a life that is lucrative, fulfilling, and rewarding.

Ambitious students can narrow down extracurricular activities until they discover what interests them most. It's better to concentrate on being committed to a few long-term pursuits rather than spreading yourself thin on too many activities. Focus on your passion. Keep in mind that in everyday life, leaders are needed in a variety of fields—from astronomy to zoology.

Some young women excel in politics. They seek out elected positions such as president of the student body or a sports team captain. Other make the most of their abilities by joining honor societies and other intellectual pursuits. Still others prefer to target specific areas of interest. They may spend their spare time as newspaper editors, band members, artists, chess players, computer enthusiasts, environmental activists, debate captains, or directors of school plays.

SPORTS TEAMS

Joining a sports team is a great way for girls to gain, sharpen, and demonstrate their leadership skills. Girls are no longer relegated to the sidelines, where their role in the past was largely to cheer for the boys. With the passage of legislation in 1972 mandating gender equality in school activities, including sports, women have moved onto the playing field, giving them a chance to display their natural competitive spirit.

Female athletes are setting records in high school and college sports that were previously off-limits, such as basketball and soccer. Some ambitious athletes

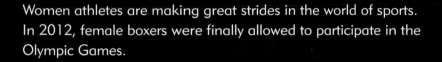

Women athletes are making great strides in the world of sports. In 2012, female boxers were finally allowed to participate in the Olympic Games.

continue their athletic participation after graduation by playing professional sports. They are scoring successes in Women's World Cup soccer and the Women's National Basketball Association. They are winning medals in Olympic games that were traditionally male, such as ice hockey and weight lifting. The last holdout—boxing—finally allowed women to fight for the gold at the 2012 Olympics.

Playing team sports helps women to build their self-esteem. These athletes also acquire other valuable traits that empower them to become leaders, such as how to manage time, make tough decisions, abide by rules, and cooperate with teammates and opponents.

A national program called GoGirlGo! focuses on sports to give girls ages eight through eighteen "the confidence they need to become the next generation of healthy and successful leaders," according to its website. Through the Women's Sports Foundation it offers grants to teams that show leadership in their communities. Teams plan community projects designed to improve girls' sports and physical activity programs in their neighborhoods. The grants fund athletic equipment, coaching, scholarships, travel, and league fees.

AFTER-SCHOOL ACTIVITIES

In addition to playing sports, girls can hone leadership skills by joining after-school activities, clubs, or community service projects. Some girls learn about a community issue and then develop and conduct a plan of action.

Teens can easily search for leadership programs in their communities. Start by seeking out news of upcoming opportunities that interest you. Read your school and community newspapers to find events you may participate in. Contact local volunteer organizations to discover how you can get involved. Ask your guidance counselor and female business leaders if they can recommend any community service projects where you could develop your leadership potential. Conduct searches on the internet to see if there are any leadership opportunities in your school or community that you may have overlooked.

Perhaps you will take an active role in your community by creating your own leadership opportunities. Focus on an issue that you are passionate about, such as the environment. Find a problem and brainstorm a solution. Then involve others to get the ball rolling. You could publicize the issue through posters, newspaper press releases, and networking. For example, you may organize teams to pick up trash on the beach or start a community garden to raise produce for the local soup kitchen.

COMMUNITY ACTION

Across the country, and beyond, young women are making changes in their own backyards. One leadership program, Girls for a Change (GFC), empowers girls to create social change. This organization inspires girls to realize their full potential by helping them develop confidence in their voices and convictions.

Her Majesty
Queen Rania

cman

GFC invites young women "to design, lead, fund and implement social change projects that tackle issues girls face in their own neighborhoods." This social change organization connects girls with volunteer female coaches who act as role models. Together, they aim to create an environment "where girls with strong voices become active leaders and passionately engaged citizens, impacting not only their own neighborhoods but also their nations as girls become informed and participating citizens in their civic, political and cultural communities."

In US cities and five countries, Girl Action Teams are transforming the world. These future leaders' mission is to make lasting changes in their neighborhoods, cities, and schools.

Another after-school program also provides opportunities for girls to become leaders. The Young Women's Leadership Alliance (YWLA) recruits high school girls ages fourteen through seventeen for their leadership capacity. Participants also develop skills in subjects such as science, social studies, and technology that they can apply to future college and career goals.

These young women reported an increase of leadership skills upon completion of the program. Their confidence surged. They became more assertive, outgoing, and outspoken. They were able to work in group settings with a variety of people and to stand up for their causes.

MAKING A DIFFERENCE

Other students team up with classmates and friends, or work alone to make a difference. They know that throughout history, the power of ordinary people can change the world in extraordinary ways.

Girls across America are leading by example, volunteering countless hours of service. They've presented workshops that focus on accessing higher education resources for immigrant high school students and their families. They've held rallies to help end violence against women, lining up guest speakers, community resources, and self-defense workshops. They've created public service announcements to help combat child abuse. They've started animal shelters for unwanted dogs and sanctuaries for former race and work horses. They've raised funds to help protect

police dogs by donating bulletproof vests to keep these canine heroes safe. They've collected signatures and founded Teens Against Whaling to end commercial whaling worldwide. They've become trailblazers, speaking out and helping change laws that require students to dissect animals. They've started Save Our Stream to protect the brook trout's habitat and formed Change the World Kids to safeguard endangered animals in the Costa Rican rain forest.

These ambitious girls have adult role models for leadership. They include parents and other relatives, teachers, guidance counselors, coaches, religious leaders, and directors of youth clubs and organizations. According to the Girl Scout Research Institute, girls don't rate celebrities high on the scale as positive influences on their leadership ambitions. Only a few media personalities, such as Oprah Winfrey, made the grade as examples to emulate. With celebrity scandals and personal crises in the headlines, girls view these famous people with "disappointment and weariness." It is therefore a good idea to look to the inspirational women in one's own life—and one's own community— as leadership role models.

MYTHS AND
FACTS

MYTH: Women aren't natural leaders.

FACT: Anybody can become a leader, although some individuals are born with more natural aptitude than others. However, men are not naturally better leaders than women. Rather, in many societies women have been socialized to better use leadership skills, such as effective communication and listening.

MYTH: Women don't work as hard as men do.

FACT: According to a 2016 study by the World Economic Forum, women typically work one hour longer each day then men when care-taking duties are included. This extra hour a day adds up to nearly forty extra days a month of work.

MYTH: There are fewer women in the workforce, which is why fewer women hold leadership positions.

FACT: In the United States, women make up 47 percent of the workforce—or nearly half of all workers. Yet, women hold significantly fewer leadership positions. This is not due to a lack of desire or of women removing themselves from the workforce, but rather a lack of opportunity provided in many companies for women to take on leadership roles.

CHAPTER 4

FEMALE CORPORATE LEADERS

Over the past fifty years, women have taken on expanding roles in the United States—and the global—workforce. According to the US Bureau of Labor Statistics, 57 percent of women in the United States are employed. The American workforce is made up of 47 percent women, or slightly less than 50 percent parity with men. Women also make up approximately 40 percent of the global workforce, according to the World Bank. While the increase of women's participation in the workforce is encouraging, there are still many challenges that they face globally. In particular, while women are employed at relatively high rates,

Meg Whitman is the former CEO of eBay and the current CEO of Hewlett-Packard. She has been named one of the world's most powerful women in business.

they often are denied the positions, promotions, and pay that men achieve in their careers. For example, although they hold nearly 52 percent of all professional-level jobs in the United States, the number of women who hold chief executive officer (CEO) positions remains stagnant at 14.6 percent. This number dives down to 4.6 percent of CEOs in Fortune 500 companies.

These statistics show the dire consequences that many women face in the workforce as they attempt to reach higher ranks in the corporate world. Those who occupy the C-Suite consist of corporations' most influential individuals—the C-Suite is used to collectively refer to a corporation's important senior executives, whose titles tend to start with the letter C, for *chief*, as in chief executive officer. C-Suite executives earn much higher salaries than other corporate workers and have greater influence in the paths their corporations take. Today, women are slowly trickling into this traditionally male-dominated space.

CORPORATE WOMEN AT THE TOP

These successful female leaders are transforming American businesses in the twenty-first century. They have seized opportunities and promoted their accomplishments as they climbed to the top of the corporate ladder. The following are a few leaders who are worth emulating.

MEG WHITMAN (EBAY, HEWLETT-PACKARD)

Meg Whitman, the former CEO of eBay, was ranked by *Fortune* magazine as the world's third-most-powerful woman in business. She helped build the eBay brand, growing the online auction site from a startup with thirty employees into an eight-billion-dollar company with fifteen thousand employees. Now she heads computer company Hewlett-Packard in an attempt to turn around this American icon.

Whitman's mother pushed her to try new challenges, explaining that "the things that are worth doing will be hard, but if you don't try, you'll never know if you can do them." Whitman said her mother emphasized that "the price of inaction can be far greater than making a mistake—which you can almost always fix." Another leadership lesson Whitman learned from her mother was that she didn't have to be perfect, but she should never be timid.

NAOMI EARP (EEOC)

Naomi Earp, the former chair of the US Equal Employment Opportunity Commission (EEOC), is another bold woman. She recalled that her presidential appointment made her realize that she had the potential to leave a legacy. "The responsibilities," she recalled, "were awesome. As chair, I could never muse over ideas in public for fear they'd be reported as policies."

Earp's recipe for leadership success is what she calls "PIE": performance, image, and exposure. "Performance is how you do what you do. Image is how you look doing what you do. And exposure is who saw what you did and what consequence is there for what you did."

ROXANNE SPILLETT (BOYS & GIRLS CLUBS OF AMERICA)

Roxanne Spillett, the former president and CEO of Boys & Girls Clubs of America, also had tremendous responsibilities. She oversaw more than fifty thousand employees and two hundred thousand board and program volunteers. Under her leadership, the nonprofit youth organization doubled in size and tripled its revenue.

Newsweek named Spillett as one of the "15 People Who Make America Great." Her ability to make good financial judgments and quick decisions, along with her vision and dedication, contributed to her legacy. Retired General and former Secretary of State Colin Powell, a member of the club's Board of Governors, said he "never failed to be impressed by the thoughtful, strategic leadership" Spillett demonstrated, citing her three-D's: "relentless drive, discipline and determination."

Under the leadership of Roxanne Spillett, the former president and CEO of Boys & Girls Clubs of America, the nonprofit youth organization expanded to its current size.

SHERYL SANDBERG (FACEBOOK)

Another woman who embodies these three-D's is Sheryl Sandberg, the chief operating officer (COO) of Facebook. This billionaire helped steer the social network to dizzying heights. Powerful mentors assisted Sandberg as she rose to the top, and now she is repaying that good deed by acting as a role model

Sheryl Sandberg, the COO of Facebook, is one of the most powerful women in business. Her work outside of Facebook focuses on empowering women in the workforce.

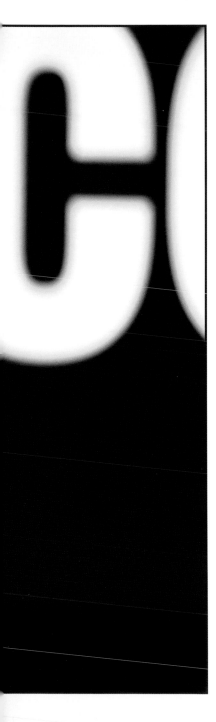

for other women in business. Her book *Lean In*: *Women, Work, and the Will to Lead*, sparked an important conversation about how to empower women in the workforce. The book also led to the creation of the Lean In Foundation, an organization that focuses on "offering women the ongoing inspiration and support to help them achieve their goals."

Sandberg advises women to aim high and "keep your foot on the gas pedal." In 2012, *Time* magazine named Sandberg one of the one hundred most powerful people in the world.

ANDREA JUNG (AVON, GRAMEEN AMERICA)

Andrea Jung, the former CEO of Avon Products, was named one of the fifty most powerful women in business by *Fortune* magazine. She formulated a turnaround plan for the eight-billion-dollar beauty

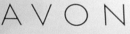

Andrea Jung worked on many philanthropic projects during her tenure as the CEO of Avon Products, including starting campaigns to end violence against women.

company, expanding it overseas. Under her oversight, Avon took a leading role in campaigns to end violence against women through the Avon Foundation for Women. Her work for this organization earned Jung the 2010 Clinton Global Citizen Award and the Avon Foundation for Women is often cited as the largest women-focused philanthropy organization in the world.

In 2014, Jung took on a new role as CEO of Grameen America, a nonprofit microfinance organization. This organization provides loans and other financial incentives for women in poverty who would like to begin small businesses. Under Jung's time at Grameen, it has become one of the fastest-growing microfinance organizations in the United States.

Jung's leadership talent lies in her extraordinary popularity with her employees and her ability to inspire them. Communication "face to face, not in an e-mail" is one of her key methods to maintaining employee morale.

Another technique she has used is to constantly reinvent herself. "Fire yourself on a Friday night and come in on Monday morning as if a search firm put you there as a turn-around leader," Jung recommended. "I'm not the same leader I was even last year, because those skills have rendered themselves not as useful."

THE IMPORTANCE OF FEMALE MENTORS

For young women who would like to emulate these leaders in the future, pairing up with a powerful female mentor is an important step. With her years of experience, a mentor can help guide younger women on their journeys through school, college, and into the career world. She will offer advice and support while watching over and fostering progress.

One way to find such a mentor is by focusing on a variety of passion-based mentoring programs in existence. For example, Girls Write Now (GWN) combines mentoring and writing instruction. This program serves high-school girls in New York City by providing guidance, support, and opportunities for future writers. GWN's mission is "to develop their creative, independent voices, explore careers in professional writing, and learn how to make healthy school, career and life choices."

GWN boasts a roster of female mentors, including essayists, journalists, playwrights, poets, and novelists. This inspiring team has empowered nearly six thousand teenage girls to find their voices as writers. Each teen is matched with a mentor, and the pair meets weekly until the teen graduates high school. Together they attend cultural events and write and edit essays, plays, poems, and stories. The strongest writing is showcased in an annual anthology.

College-prep mentorship is geared toward high school students navigating the college pathway. These programs foster student leadership while increasing educational expectations. For example, high school students in the Sponsor-a-Scholar program in Philadelphia improved their grades and enrolled in colleges at higher rates than students who lacked access to a mentor. Students discover how to connect with a college, set scholastic and career goals, and explore careers with mentors who offer support and motivation.

The word "mentor" comes from the Greek for "steadfast" and "enduring." According to GWN, having a mentor "is the most significant, indisputable factor in keeping teenagers off the streets and helping them reach college and overcome poverty." Girls who participate in a mentoring program have improved "relationships with parents, school value, scholastic abilities, grades, and attendance rates."

MENTOR, the National Mentoring Partnership, points out that only three million out of eighteen million young people have a caring adult in their lives. Teens who are searching for a mentorship program may start by talking to relatives, friends' mothers, teachers, guidance counselors, and leaders at religious or neighborhood organizations such as Big Brothers Big Sisters.

Along with face-to-face interactions with mentors, there are e-mentors who offer advice and guidance via chat or email. For example, 1,500 volunteers from a wide range of fields connect with middle- and high-school students in a program called iCouldBe. They act as cheerleaders, supporting students as they prepare for college and careers—all through fostering relationships online. These mentors help guide teens toward success, offer advice to surmount obstacles, and help teens achieve their goals.

FEMALE ENTREPRENEURS

An increasing number of women are getting ahead by starting at the top. Female-owned businesses have grown in number, size, and profitability. Women across the world are turning their passions into profits. They are busy inventing, creating, solving, selling, and consulting through their own businesses.

The trials and tribulations of self-employment are not for the faint of heart. If you wish to become a successful entrepreneur, start taking the first steps while still in school. Focus on courses that will help you to build your future empire, such as business, marketing, and financing.

Anita Roddick founded the Body Shop, which grew into
a global business that now serves seventy-seven million

Approximately 90 percent of teachers and guidance counselors say that their students are interested in becoming entrepreneurs, according to a survey by Young Entrepreneur Foundation. The foundation has started a new curriculum for high-school students called "Entrepreneur in the Classroom." It focuses on the foundations of business theory, developing business ideas, and how to run a business. The foundation also recruits local entrepreneurs to serve as inspiring mentors.

Another high-school program challenges students in grades nine through twelve to develop a business plan. After completing seven sessions, students who enroll in the JA Be Entrepreneurial program set up their own commercial enterprises while still in high school. Students learn a variety of leadership skills, such as how to develop innovative thinking skills, analyze and present information, make decisions, work in groups, and express multiple viewpoints. They discover how successful entrepreneurs funded projects on tight budgets, how they developed their products and services ideas, and how they grew their businesses.

You may be inspired by the savvy women profiled in this chapter, who lead thriving entrepreneurial ventures. They took risks, exercised initiative, seized opportunities, and emerged on top.

OPRAH (OWN)

Perhaps the most successful woman who has built her own empire is Oprah Winfrey. This billionaire has appeared on various media lists as the most powerful woman in the world. Her television talk show, which aired more than five thousand broadcasts, catapulted its host into fame and fortune. Winfrey became the highest-paid television performer, the wealthiest self-made woman in America, and the richest African American of the twentieth century.

This industry and entertainment leader believes that "you have a responsibility to yourself to learn as much about your business as you can." A secret to her success, Winfrey says, is "I have people that I trust. I also try to surround myself with people who are smarter than I am. I think that the ability to be as good as you can be comes from understanding who you are, and what you can and cannot do."

She also advises, "It doesn't matter who you are, where you come from. The ability to triumph begins with you. Always."

ANITA RODDICK (THE BODY SHOP)

Anita Roddick also was victorious after setting up the Body Shop to create a livelihood for her family. Her tiny, handmade cosmetics shop grew to more than 2,045 stores serving seventy-seven million customers.

She ran her business ethically, with what she called moral leadership. Roddick linked her products with corporate activism by promoting causes such as human rights, the environment, and ending animal testing.

Nicknamed the "queen of green," she believed in "having a passion to shout out and be persuasive about what you do." Her "cosmetics with a conscience" set the Body Shop apart from its competitors and made Roddick one of the richest women in England. This business leader believed in speaking out for her causes, which attracted a loyal following. "If you think you're too small to have an impact, try going to bed with a mosquito," she advised.

DEBBI FIELDS (MRS. FIELD'S COOKIES)

Debbi Fields also achieved the American Dream when she launched her dessert company. She built her company from scratch, starting with a recipe for chocolate chip cookies. Mrs. Fields Cookies became a brand symbol, a franchise with more than six hundred stores, and a $450 million empire.

Her company's reputation is reflected in her motto: "Good Enough Never Is." Despite naysayers, Fields pursued her passion by blending determination, innovation, and self-confidence. "The greatest failure is not to try," she explained. "Had I listened to all the people during the course of my life who said, 'You can't. You'll fail. It won't work. You don't have …,' I wouldn't be here today."

MARTINE ALIANA ROTHBLATT

Martine Aliana Rothblatt's mother remembers holding her a newborn and understanding the difference her child would make in the world. "I remember saying … 'I don't know what it is, but there's something special about you. You will make a difference in this world.' And she is."

(continued on the next page)

Martine Rothblatt is currently the highest-paid CEO in the United States. She has built up many important technology companies, such as SiriusXM, all while staying true to herself.

(continued from the previous page)

Rothblatt is currently the highest-paid CEO in the United States. She began her career as a lawyer representing the television broadcasting industry. Later, she pursued graduate studies in astronomy and worked for the National Aeronautics and Space Administration (NASA). In the late 1980s, Rothblatt was the CEO of innovative global telecommunications satellite company Geostar Corporation. She left Geostar to begin her own corporation—Sirius Satellite Radio, now known as SiriusXM. Today, Rothblatt is the founder and CEO of United Therapeutics, a biotechnology company that develops innovative medical technology.

In 1994, Rothblatt came out as a trans woman. She remembers that some of her business partners could not accept her gender identity. "There were business associations who would have nothing further to do with me," she said. "[They] just cut me off completely." But Rothblatt persevered. She has since become a vocal advocate for trans rights and one of the most innovative entrepreneurs in the world.

According to Judy Olian, dean of the UCLA Anderson School of Management, "the essence of this renaissance thinker, trailblazing innovator and very successful doer [is] four qualities … First, she is a pragmatic problem solver … Second, she is a leader who inspires others with her authenticity … Third, her curiosity and hunger for creative ideas are evident in every conversation … [And] fourth, Rothblatt is a powerful communicator."

ALEXANDRA SCOTT (ALSF)

Another inspiring young woman started a lemonade stand in her front yard and used all her proceeds to battle childhood cancer. When Alexandra Scott was four years old and battling pediatric cancer, she told her mother that as soon as she left the hospital, she wanted to open her stand to raise money so doctors could help other sick kids.

Alex's first stand raised two thousand dollars and spurred Alex's Lemonade Stand Foundation for Childhood Cancer (ALSF). She and her family continued to raise funds with an annual lemonade stand. Alex inspired people around the world to host their own stands and donate the proceeds to her cause.

Sadly, Alex lost her battle at the age of eight. Her unique charity, whose motto is "fighting childhood cancer, one cup at a time," continues her legacy. Alex's Lemonade Stand Foundation has raised more than $140 million, funding more than 690 research projects nationally.

RACHEL ZIETZ (GLADIATOR LACROSSE)

In 2013, thirteen-year-old lacrosse player Rachel Zietz grew frustrated with finding equipment that would last intense rounds of practice. So she began her own company, Gladiator Lacrosse. Zietz was inspired from the entrepreneurship in her own family—her mother and father began their own merchant services business—and from participating in the thirty-three-week Young Entrepreneur's Academy. Following this teen entrepreneur program, she pitched her idea and won $2,700 to begin her company, which, as of 2017, has profits in excess of $2 million annually.

Zietz credits her success with acting in a confident and respectful way in all of her business dealings. She says, "People don't treat me like a kid; they treat me like a business woman." She also advises, "It's never too young to start. I started when I was thirteen, and it was successful. Most people are afraid, but if you're passionate about it, you're never too young."

CHAPTER 5

POWERFUL POLITICAL WOMEN

Although women still make up a smaller share of political leaders around the world, this doesn't mean that women haven't historically influenced politics in very big ways.

Hillary Clinton made history when she became the first woman in the United States to win a presidential nomination from a major political party.

Many of the most influential political leaders in history have been women, such as Russian empress Catherine the Great, Indian prime minister Indira Gandhi, and British prime minister Margaret Thatcher.

Female political leaders can help create positive social change. When more women are elected into office, they help ensure more voices are heard in policy decisions. While a woman has yet to be elected president or vice president of the United States, female political leaders are actively attaining firsts. In 2016, Hillary Clinton made history when she became the first female presidential candidate to win a nomination from a major US political party. Although she won the majority of the popular vote, she did not win the electoral votes to become the first female president of the United States.

FEMALE POLITICAL LEADERS

In the 115th Congress, women hold twenty-one seats in the US Senate and 83 seats in the US House of Representatives, totaling 104 women out of the 535 voting members. In the 42nd Canadian Parliament, a record number of female lawmakers were elected with 88 women elected to the House of Commons. Globally, approximately 23 percent of members of national parliaments are women. This number has been gradually on the rise from 11 percent in 1995.

While the United States lags behind other countries in terms of women in political office, many American female politicians have paved the way for future political leaders both in the United States and abroad.

GERALDINE FERRARO

Geraldine Ferraro ended the male-dominated national politics when she became the first female vice president candidate representing a major American political party. The former Queens congresswoman accepted the Democratic nomination in 1984. She and presidential candidate Walter Mondale failed to win a victory.

This historical first-timer broke down the barriers and gave women hope to someday occupy the Oval Office. Ferraro's nomination came sixty-four years after women won the right to vote. She later served as US ambassador to the United Nations Human Rights Commission.

Mondale called his running mate "a gutsy pioneer who stood up and fought for America to open its door to all Americans, including women." In the 1980s, he noted, "America was changing. The culture of our country had been very restrictive toward women, even women of great talent, by putting them in a box."

NANCY PELOSI

Another remarkable female politician, Nancy Pelosi, also made history when she was elected as the first woman to serve as Speaker of the House. "I stood on the shoulders of those who have come before me—Susan B. Anthony, Elizabeth Cady Stanton, Alice Paul, Sojourner Truth—and every other pioneer who fought to gain the right to vote and empowerment for women," Pelosi said.

The *Christian Science Monitor* called Pelosi "the most powerful woman in American politics." As the Democratic Leader of the US House of Representatives, this tough-minded and aggressive chief inspired others to make things happen. *The Washington Post* said Pelosi was "on a mission to smash the old-boy network in Washington."

Pelosi's leadership style includes being a good listener, bringing people together, and keeping her followers in the loop with one-on-one meetings. "I do try to have decisions made in a collegial way. Listening and talking it through rather than just deciding how something will be or conducting a meeting in a way that doesn't elicit honest response," she explained.

CONDOLEEZZA RICE

Condoleezza Rice was the first woman to serve at the head of the National Security Council and the first African American woman to serve as secretary of state. Prior to her stint in politics, Rice also broke two records in education: the first female and first African

Condoleezza Rice was the first African American woman to serve as secretary of state in the United States. She went on to break many other barriers to women in politics.

American to become a provost, or high-ranking administrative officer, of Stanford University.

This leader, who grew up during the civil rights movement in segregated Birmingham, Alabama, was inspired to lead by her college professor parents. "My parents," said Rice, "had me absolutely convinced that, well, you may not be able to have a hamburger at Woolworth's but you can be president of the United States."

SANDRA DAY O'CONNOR

Trailblazer Sandra Day O'Connor became the first female justice appointed to the United States Supreme Court in its 191-year history. In 1981, when the Republican was sworn in, she broke new ground for women in the legal field. O'Connor, who served for twenty-four years, said, "The power I exert on the court depends on the power of my arguments, not on my gender."

The Supreme Court justice had come a long way from her law school graduation in 1952. Despite being at the top of her class, O'Connor could not find a job as a lawyer because of discrimination against women. "Despite the encouraging and wonderful gains and the changes for women which have occurred in my lifetime," she said, "there is still room to advance and to promote correction of the remaining deficiencies and imbalances."

HILLARY CLINTON

Another female leader politician who rocketed to national prominence, Hillary Rodham Clinton, successfully combined power and politics in a variety of roles. As a lawyer, she became partner in a prestigious firm and was named one of the one hundred most powerful American lawyers by the *National Law Journal*. As a first lady, she was a dynamic, strong partner to her husband, the forty-second president of the United States, William "Bill" Clinton. As a New York senator, she set a record as the only first lady to hold a national office. In 2007, Clinton ran for the Democratic presidential nomination but conceded to Barack Obama, who won the presidency. President Obama nominated Clinton to Secretary of State in his cabinet.

Then, in 2016, Clinton set another record: the first female presidential candidate of a major US political party. Clinton won the majority of the popular vote, although she lost the electoral votes needed to win the presidency and conceded to Donald Trump.

When Clinton gave up her presidential race, she mentioned not having broken the glass ceiling. Clinton was referring to the invisible barrier that stops a woman's upward advancement because of discrimination based on her gender. However, acknowledging the nearly sixty-five million Americans who supported her presidential bid, Clinton said in her concession speech that the "highest, hardest glass ceiling" had still not been "shattered." But, she said, "some day someone will and hopefully sooner than we may think right now. And to all the little girls who are watching this, never doubt that you are valuable and powerful and deserving of every chance and opportunity in the world to pursue and achieve your own dreams."

Although her visionary leadership style didn't land Clinton in the Oval Office, and she insists she will not run again, this influential figure continues to remain positive about a woman's role as a political leader. "From now on, it will be unremarkable for a woman to win primary state victories, unremarkable to have a woman in a close race to be our nominee, unremarkable to think that a woman can be the president of the United States," she told supporters. "And that is truly remarkable."

LUBNA KHALID AL QASIMI

Born in the United Arab Emirates (UAE) in 1962, Lubna Khalid Al Qasimi has held numerous roles in the Emirati government. After earning a bachelor's

(continued on page 80)

Lubna Khalid Al Qasimi has held many governmental roles in the United Arab Emirates. She was also a successful CEO of the global corporation Tejari.

(continued from page 78)

degree in computer science and an Executive MBA, Al Qasimi become CEO of Tejari, a Middle Eastern business-to-business marketplace. Under Al Qasimi's leadership, Tejari increased its sales and was given the World Summit for Information Society's award for one of the best e-business providers.

But Al Qasimi was not content to remain in the corporate world. In 2000, she became the first woman in her country's history to be appointed to a cabinet position when she was named Minister of Economy, a position she held until 2004. From 2004 until 2016, Al Qasimi was Minister of State for International Cooperation, where she led the UAE into "a period of unprecedented philanthropy," according to *Forbes* magazine. As of 2016, Al Qasimi has taken on a new role as Minister of Tolerance, in which she brings together UAE politicians with other global leaders in diplomatic missions. She was named one of the world's fifty most powerful women by *Forbes*. Al Qasimi has stated, "I am a firm believer that the true progress of a society or a nation can be determined by the way it treats women. Progressive thinking and economic prosperity are meaningless unless women are given the respect and honor they deserve."

FUTURE FEMALE POLITICAL LEADERS

How can more female leaders be encouraged to enter politics? Similar to methods that jump-start a business career, mentoring and networking are keys to victory. Future female leaders should seek out successful women in politics and request mentoring. Another tactic is to research how these women won elections by reading their speeches, exploring their organizational activities, and scrutinizing their political platforms.

Political hopefuls should also search for any networking opportunities on the political scene, such as campaign fundraisers, conferences, and lobbying. There, female leaders can ask other women to share resources and strategies on how to enter the political arena.

One organization that fosters female candidates in the United States is EMILY's List. In 1985, the twenty-five "founding mothers" networked using old-fashioned Rolodexes to contact friends about raising money for pro-choice female Democratic candidates. These political leaders have since raised more than five million dollars and encompass a community of more than five million.

Their goal is "connecting women and electing women to make progressive change." EMILY's List searches for viable political opportunities and then recruits female candidates for positions as congresswomen and governors. It raises funds for their campaigns and provides training so the candidates have the winning edge. The organization conducts research "into the minds and moods of women voters" and reaches out to get these voters to go to the polls and cast their ballots for the candidates EMILY's List has spotlighted.

The organization is making a difference by changing the face of American politics and inspiring change in other nations. "The global impact of women in leadership positions is every bit as exciting as what's happening on the national stage," said Jessica McIntosh, a spokeswoman for EMILY's List. "The more young women and girls can look up to women in power, the more likely they are to see themselves holding such a job."

EMPOWERING FEMALE LEADERS

It may seem daunting to young women to figure out how to navigate the leadership maze and triumph. But there are easy steps to take in order to build leadership skills and follow a path to success. When entering the workforce, it is important to seek out female mentors for advice and support. It is also important for young women to choose careers that match their values and interests—it is hard to develop leadership skills in a field you don't feel passionately about.

A young woman on the career track needs to do her homework when it comes to searching for that first job.

For young women interested in taking on leadership positions in the professional world, it is important to develop networking skills.

She should focus on a company that both values and promotes women. She should investigate whether women are given responsibility early in their position, which allows them to achieve their top potential. The new professional should take charge and become the CEO of her career, guaranteeing both personal and professional success.

NETWORKING FOR SUCCESS

On her journey toward getting hired, a young professional woman needs to network to get new doors to open in every direction. She should attend events where she can meet and make connections with people in her field who could help her during early career stages. She should invest her time wisely by going to chamber of commerce breakfasts, alumni events, career fairs, and trade shows. She may also connect with online networks via social media sites.

To maximize future leadership success, the young woman should aspire to act professionally in all of her networking endeavors. She should dress as if she was going on a formal job interview. She should come equipped with resumes and business cards. To make a professional first impression, she should stand tall, shake hands, make eye contact, smile, speak clearly, ask questions, and listen. A thank-you note after networking events will help her to stand out from the competition.

SEEKING—AND BECOMING—A MENTOR

Once the internship or job is secured, a good mentor can help an intern or employee acclimate to her new work environment. A professional mentoring relationship can last throughout a young professional's entire career. Search for a mentor who has experience in your field, such as a former professor or a family friend. Again, social media sites can help you connect and mingle with mentors in an industry-specific online community.

In the beginning stages, a mentor can both advise and support, alleviating stress. Mentors can introduce young women to others within the industry or organization. They can help new professionals develop their careers while overcoming obstacles

Seeking out a mentor is another way young women can develop their leadership skills and advance their careers.

and barriers. Mentors can point young women in the right direction, guide them down the correct career path, and help them build their networks. Mentors can offer personally tailored advice from their insider positions.

As the young professional gains power and is promoted up the business ladder, she needs to help the next generation of women to follow in her footsteps on the path to leadership. Instead of feeling threatened by or competing with female coworkers, she needs to cooperate with and support them. This is when she can become a mentor herself, helping to hire and promote young women who are just starting their careers. On her lifelong journey to becoming an exceptional leader, the young career woman should start mentoring protégées. She will grow professionally as she shares information and challenges with new future female leaders.

Today's young women look ahead to the future in anticipation that they will hold positions of leadership in direct proportion to men. Only then will colleagues respond to these female leaders in terms of their capabilities and skills, with their gender becoming less relevant.

TAPPING WOMEN'S FULL POTENTIAL

Companies need to tap the full potential of working women in order for them to ascend to the leadership pinnacles of corporate America. A Women in the Economy report sponsored by the *Wall Street Journal* explored the challenges women face and offered solutions. According to the report, "Corporate America has a leaky talent pipeline: At each transition up the management ranks, more women are left behind."

To start, Women in the Economy stressed that corporations should recruit their fair share or more of women. Then, to keep their female employees, they should offer flexible work arrangements. Many companies have transformed into family-friendly workplaces. They provide parents of both sexes with parental leaves and work schedules that accommodate families. Some employees opt for flextime, a system

that allows them to set their own daily times of starting and finishing work. Others decide on job-sharing, the dividing up of the responsibilities of a single full-time job between two or more part-time workers. Still others select telecommuting, working from home on a personal computer linked to the workplace.

Other barriers that are holding women back need to be addressed, Women in the Economy emphasized. The report discovered, through research and interviews, that intelligent, highly motivated women in middle management are turning down opportunities for advancement. Many of these women believe that the odds of getting ahead are too daunting. They remain at their current levels for a variety of reasons, including "not having a sponsor in upper management to create opportunities."

The most powerful force stopping female candidates from advancing is ingrained beliefs. Managers of both genders, the report found, take these women "out of the running, often on the assumption that the woman can't handle certain jobs and also discharge family obligations."

A woman's own mindset, as well, can limit her opportunities. She may be waiting to be asked to move forward in rank or position. Or she may believe that she needs additional skills, training, and experience before attempting to advance. She may disqualify *herself* because she doesn't think she has the capacity to lead others successfully.

Working women at a stalemate could benefit from a shot of self-esteem. They can gain confidence in their own merit through career advancing strategies. They should seek out strong, supportive role models and join mentoring programs. When young women see other women holding top positions, they realize the possibilities that are available. They begin to believe, "If she can be a successful leader, then so can I."

Career women should also make important connections through work-related social activities. They should choose alternatives, such as executive coaching and training in a women-only environment. These approaches can help women to market and promote themselves and their ideas.

The report emphasized how companies can unlock the full potential of working women. Businesses need to help qualified women to grow, develop, and advance, focusing especially on the shift from mid-level manager to senior management. Women in middle management are aiming for top roles, such as vice president. They have the ambition and confidence to succeed as leaders. If companies would advance 25 percent of these women to the next level, it would dramatically change the shape of that leaky talent pipeline.

Finding meaning in work is motivation for many successful

FIVE INGREDIENTS FOR SUCCESS

The McKinsey Centered Leadership Project strives to help develop women leaders. Project consultants Joanna Barsh and Susie Cranston describe in their book, *How Remarkable Women Lead: The Breakthrough Model for Work and Life*, five key ingredients as a recipe for leading a more successful life. By focusing on these elements, the authors claim that female employees "have a far greater likelihood of achieving success in three important outcomes: Passion for work, effectiveness as a leader, and satisfaction in life."

The first and most important key on the road to leadership is *meaning*. Meaningful work motivates the successful woman. Her job becomes her calling. She starts with her personal strengths and matches them to a job that is the right fit. She discovers that when she is passionate about her job, happiness will follow. A happy leader is more productive, creative, and effective. Instead of passively waiting for her life to change, she makes things happen.

The second key is positive *framing*. The female leader needs to view situations optimistically. By remaining flexible, she is open to new possibilities and ideas. She isn't stuck in a routine and finds risk exciting. She adapts to new challenges and sees opportunity in setbacks. She can move ahead by turning mistakes and obstacles into opportunities for growth. After she identifies the problem she can take action.

The third key is *connecting*. The female leader who builds meaningful relationships inspires others. Being a part of a team leads to greater success. The woman who connects with strong networks and mentors, according to the authors, enjoys "more promotions, higher pay, and greater work satisfaction." Remember, nobody does it alone.

The fourth key is *engaging*. The successful leader seizes opportunities to make things happen. Despite risks and fears, she finds the courage to speak up. Developing the confidence to discover her voice can help her to become an ambitious decision-maker.

The fifth and final key is *energizing*. Leadership pressures are exhausting. The female leader needs to minimize energy drains. She needs to constantly restore her energy by exercising, eating nutritious meals, and getting enough sleep. If she's running on empty, she may make bad choices. If she's energized, she will get excited about the future.

10
GREAT QUESTIONS

TO ASK A FEMALE MENTOR

Having a good relationship with a mentor is one of the best advantages a young women looking to develop her leadership skills can have. Young women can glean advice from the inspiring mentors in their lives by asking the following questions:

1. What can I do to prepare for a career in this field?

2. How have you balanced a demanding career with your personal life?

3. What would you have done differently in the early stages of your career?

4. What long-term and short-term goals should I have in order to become a leader?

5. What can I do to guarantee that I will continue to grow and develop as a leader?

6. What are some challenges that emerging leaders face?

7. How has networking gotten you to where you are today?

8. What would you suggest is the most effective way to network?

9. What advice can you offer me as I go into my first leadership position?

10. Who are other leaders you recommend that I contact?

FUTURE FEMALE LEADERS OF THE WORLD UNITE!

Young women growing up today find themselves in an exciting time in history. Young women have more opportunities than ever before. In particular, women today are more likely than men to attend college and to earn graduate degrees in the United States. American women in their thirties are also more likely to become doctors and lawyers than in any other generation before them. While, both in North America and abroad, women face many obstacles to achieving full parity with men, there is reason to hope. According to the Center for American Progress, it may take until 2085 for women to achieve full parity with men in countries, such as the United States—but determined and dedicated young women are fighting to achieve this goal faster every day.

ABOLITION The official ending of the practice of slavery during the eighteenth and nineteenth centuries.

ASSERTIVE Having or showing self-confidence while not being afraid to make one's needs known.

CEO Acronym for chief executive officer; the highest-ranking manager in a company.

CHARISMA The ability to inspire enthusiasm, interest, or affection in others by means of personal charm or influence.

CISGENDER Used to describe a person whose gender identity matches with the sex they were assigned at birth.

COMPORTMENT The particular way in which someone behaves.

CONCEDE To accept and acknowledge defeat in a contest, debate, or election.

C-SUITE Used to collectively refer to a corporation's most important senior executives, whose titles tend to start with the letter C, for "chief," as in chief executive officer.

DEMURE The act of being reserved, modest, or shy.

EMPATHY The ability to identify with and understand another person's feelings

ENTREPRENEUR Someone who sets up and finances new commercial enterprises to make a profit.

FORTUNE 500 A list of the 500 largest companies in the United States, compiled annually by the business magazine *Fortune*.

GLASS CEILING An invisible but real barrier within a hierarchy that prevents qualified women from obtaining upper-level positions.

LOBBY To attempt to persuade a political representative to support or fight a particular case.

MENTOR Somebody, usually older and more experienced, who provides advice and support to, watches over, and fosters the progress of a younger and less experienced person.

PARITY The state or condition of being equal, especially in terms of status or pay.

PATRIARCHAL Used to describe a society or government controlled by men.

SOCIAL INTELLIGENCE The ability to form rewarding relationships with other people.

SUFFRAGE The right to vote in public elections.

TRAILBLAZER A pioneer or innovator in a particular field.

TRANSACTIONAL LEADERSHIP Also known as managerial leadership, this type of leadership style focuses on the roles of supervision, organization, and group performance, using the behavior of leaders to influence their staffs.

TRANSFORMATIONAL LEADERSHIP This type of leadership style creates positive changes in those who follow and in social systems, using the vision and inspiration of leaders to exert significant influence.

WEBINAR A live online educational presentation during which viewers can submit questions and comments.

WOMEN'S MOVEMENT The organized effort by women to change the ways they are perceived and treated.

The Canadian Women's Foundation
    Leadership Institute
    133 Richmond Street West, Suite 504
    Toronto, ON M5H 2L3
    Canada
(416) 365-1444
Email: info@canadianwomen.org
Facebook: @CanadianWomensFounation
The Canadian Women's Foundation Leadership
    Institute empowers women and girls in
    Canada. It aims to remove Canadian women
    and girls from violence and poverty and to
    inspire them to confidence and leadership.

Girl Scouts of the USA
    420 Fifth Avenue
    New York, NY 10018
(800) 478-7248
Website: www.girlscouts.org
Facebook: @GirlScoutsUSA
Twitter: @GirlScouts
Girl Scouts, the largest organization for girls
    in the world, provides young women with
    opportunities for fun and friendship while
    fostering the development of leadership skills
    and self-esteem. The Girl Scouts "believe in
    the power of every girl to change the world."

Girls for a Change (GFC)
  PO Box 1436
  San Jose, CA 95109
  (866) 738-4422
  Website: www.girlsforachange.org
  Facebook: @girlsforachange
  This national organization empowers girls to
    create social change. Girls for a Change
    inspires young women to design, lead,
    fund, and implement social change projects
    that tackle issues they face in their own
    neighborhoods.

Ms. Foundation for Women
  12 MetroTech Center
  26th Floor
  Brooklyn, NY 11201
  (212) 742-1653
  Website: ms.foundation.org
  Facebook: @MsFoundationForWomen
  Twitter: @msfoundation
  The Ms. Foundation for Women, established in
    1973, builds women's collective power across
    race and class to tackle the root causes of
    injustice and ignite progressive change for all.

National Organization for Women (NOW)
1100 H Street NW, Suite 300
Washington, DC 20005
(202) 628-8NOW [8669]
Website: www.now.org
Facebook: @NationalNOW
Twitter: @NationalNOW
The National Organization for Women, started
in 1966, is the largest organization of feminist
activists in the United States. NOW's website
provides a list of local chapters and news on
women's issues.

Office of Women's Business Ownership
Entrepreneurial Development
US Small Business Administration
409 Third Street SW
Washington, DC 20416
(202) 205-6673
Website: www.sba.gov/offices/headquarters/wbo
Twitter: @SBAgov
This office helps to establish and oversee a
network of women's business centers and
provides technical assistance to women who
are economically or socially disadvantaged.

Women in Leadership Foundation (WIL)
    186, 9–3151 Lakeshore Road
    Kelowna, BC V1W 3S9
    Canada
(250) 764-0009
Email: info@womeninleadership.ca
Website: www.womeninleadership.ca
Facebook: @WomenInLeadershipFoundation
The Women in Leadership Foundation creates
    inspirational programs that bring women
    together in developing their leadership skills
    and creating positive change in the future of
    women's leadership in Canada.

WEBSITES

Due to the changing nature of internet links,
Rosen Publishing has developed an online list of
websites related to the subject of this book. This
site is updated regularly. Please use this link to
access the list:

http://www.rosenlinks.com/WITW/Lead

Amoruso, Sophia. *#GirlBoss*. New York, NY: Portfolio, 2015.

Chiquet, Maureen. *Beyond the Label: Women, Leadership, and Success on Our Own Terms*. New York, NY: Harper Business, 2017.

Frankel, Lois P. *Nice Girls Don't Get the Corner Office: Unconscious Mistakes Women Make that Sabotage Their Careers*. New York, NY: Business Plus, 2014.

Kay, Katty, and Claire Shipman. *The Confidence Code: The Science and Art of Self-Assurance— What Women Should Know*. New York, NY: HarperBusiness, 2014.

Mayer, Catherine. *Attack of the 50 Ft. Women: How Gender Equality Can Save the World!* Huntington, WV: HQ, 2017.

Mobley, Sasha. *The Strong Woman Trap: A Feminist Guide for Getting Your Life Back*. New York, NY: Morgan James Publishing, 2017.

Morgan, Angie, and Courtney Lynch. *Leading from the Front: No-Excuse Tactics for Women*. New York, NY: McGraw-Hill Education, 2017.

Sandberg, Sheryl. *Lean In for Graduates*. New York, NY: Knopf, 2014.

Sandberg, Sheryl. *Lean In: Women, Work, and the Will to Lead*. New York, NY: Knopf, 2013.

Wallbridge, Daphne. *Step Up, Step Out: A Girl's Guide to Empowerment, Self-Leadership, And Success*. Pennsauken, NJ: BookBaby, 2017.

"About Us." Girls for a Change. Retrieved March
8, 2017. http://www.girlsforachange.org
/about-us.

"The Fight for Women's Suffrage." *History*.
Retrieved April 8, 2017. http://www.history
.com/topics/the-fight-for-womens-suffrage.

"Hillary Clinton's Concession Speech." *CNN
Politics*. November 9, 2016. http://www.cnn
.com/2016/11/09/politics/hillary-clinton
-concession-speech.

Marinova, Polina. "18 Under 18: Meet the Young
Innovators Who Are Changing the World."
Fortune, September 15, 2016. http://fortune
.com/2016/09/15/18-entrepreneurs-under-18
-teen-business.

Mattioli, Dana. "Ways Women Can Hold Their
Own in a Male World." *Wall Street Journal*,
November 25, 2008. http://online.wsj.com
/article/SB122756745919254459.html.

McKinsey and Company. "How Remarkable
Women Lead." Retrieved April 8, 2017. http://
www.mckinsey.com/ideas/books
/RemarkableWomen.

National Organization of Women. "History."
Retrieved April 8, 2017. http://www.now
.orgabout//history/index.html.

Olian, Judy. "How Martine Rothblatt Leapt
Boundaries in Science, Tech, and Gender."
Financial Times, January 29, 2017. https://
www.ft.com/content/0682a232-dbb6-11e6
-86ac-f253db7791c6.

Riggio, Ronald E. "Do Men and Women Lead
Differently? Who's Better?" *Psychology Today,*
March 23, 2010. http://www.psychologytoday
.com/blog/cutting-edge-leadership/201003
/do-men-and-women-lead-differently
-whos-better.

"Sheikha Lubna Al Qasimi." *Forbes.* Retrieved
April 8, 2017. https://www.forbes.com/profile
/sheikha-lubna-al-qasimi.

Smyth. Annabelle. "Women Leaders: 6 Myths
You Definitely Want to Check Out." *People
Development Magazine.* Retrieved April 8,
2017. http://peopledevelopmentmagazine
.com/2017/01/10/women-leaders.

"Statistical Overview of Women in the
Workplace." *Catalyst.* April 6, 2016. http://
www.catalyst.org/publication/219/statistical-
overview-of-women-in-the-workplace?loc=int
erstitialskip.

Torregrosa, Luisita Lopez. "No Longer Is
    Leadership a Men's Club." *New York Times,*
    October 11, 2011. http://www.nytimes
    .com/2011/10/12/us/12iht-letter12.html.
"UAE National Day: 13 Powerful Quotes from
    UAE's Innovative Leaders." *Elan.* December 2,
    2014. http://www.elanthemag.com/uae
    -national-day-12-powerful-quotes-uaes
    -innovative-leaders.
Warner, Judith. "Fact Sheet: The Women's
    Leadership Gap." Center for American
    Progress, March 7, 2014. https://www
    .americanprogress.org/issues/women
    /reports/2014/03/07/85457/fact-sheet
    -the-womens-leadership-gap.
"Women in the Economy." *Wall Street Journal.*
    April 2011. http://online.wsj.com/public/page
    /women-04112011.html.
"Women in the US Congress 2017." Center
    for American Women and Politics. *Rutgers
    University,* 2017. http://www.cawp.rutgers
    .edu/women-us-congress-2017.

ABOUT THE AUTHORS

Lena Koya is a writer and scholar who lives with her family in New York. She is the author of nearly twenty books and enjoys speaking to girls and young women about ways they can make a difference in the world.

Nancy Furstinger has held a variety of leading roles in publishing as a feature writer for a daily newspaper, a managing editor of trade and consumer magazines, and an editor at two children's book publishing houses. She is the author of numerous books. Furstinger also uses transformational leadership skills as an animal advocate, speaking up for all creatures great and small, wild and domestic.

PHOTO CREDITS

Cover Bloomberg/Getty Images; pp. 6–7, 18–19, 92-93 monkeybusinessimages/iStock/Thinkstock; pp. 10–11 julief514/ iStock/Thinkstock; pp. 14–15, 84–85 shironosov/iStock/Thinkstock; p. 24 Hulton Archive/Getty Images; p. 27 Kean Collection/Archive Photos/Getty Images; p. 31 Alberto E. Rodriguez/Getty Images; p. 34 Benoit Doppagne/AFP/Getty Images; p. 39 Wavebreakmedia Ltd/Thinkstock; p. 41 Scott Heavey/Getty Images; pp. 44–45 John Lamparski/WireImage/Getty Images; p. 47 Ari Perilstein/Getty Images; p. 51 Justin Sullivan/Getty Images; p. 55 Dale Wilcox/ WireImage/Getty Images; pp. 56–57 Jerod Harris/WireImage/Getty Images; p. 58 Dimitrios Kambouris/WireImage/Getty Images; p. 63 Gareth Davies/Getty Images; p. 47 The Washington Post/Getty Images; p. 71 Chip Somodevilla/Getty Images; p. 73 Santi Visalli/ Archive Photos/Getty Images; p. 75 Rob Kim/Getty Images; p. 79 Taylor Hill/FilmMagic/Getty Images; p. 87 Purestock/Thinkstock; p. 89 gpointstudio/iStock/Thinkstock; cover and interior pages (globe) LuckyDesigner/Shutterstock.com; cover and interior pages background designs lulias/Shutterstock.com, Dawid Lech/ Shutterstock.com, Transia Design/Shutterstock.com.

Design & Layout: Nicole Russo-Duca; Editor & Photo Research: Elizabeth Schmermund